The Virgin Mary,
Fr. Gobbi and the Year 2000

The Virgin Mary, Fr. Gobbi and the Year 2000

Paul A. Mihalik, Lt. Col. USAF (Ret.)

PUBLISHING COMPANY
P.O. Box 42028 Santa Barbara, CA 93140-2028
(800) 647-9882 • (805) 957-4893 • Fax: (805) 957-1631

The author recognizes and happily accepts that the final authority regarding the supernatural character of the quoted locutions in this book rests always and finally with the Catholic Church.

This book is dedicated to THE HOLY SPIRIT and HIS SPOUSE, OUR LADY, QUEEN OF MERCY. MAY THEIR LOVE, LIGHT, AND MERCY STRENGTHEN and PROTECT THE REMNANT.

©1998 Queenship Publishing

Library of Congress Number # 98-68707

Published by:
Queenship Publishing
P.O. Box 42028
Santa Barbara, CA 93140-2028
(800) 647-9882 • (805) 957-4893 • Fax: (805) 957-1631

Printed in the United States of America

ISBN: 1-57918-106-6

Contents

"Oh my beloved Jesus, through Thy five most precious wounds, may the souls in Purgatory find comfort and release, and through Thy most loving, generous, and Sacred Heart may sins be forgiven and sinners converted. Amen."

Introduction

This book discusses the ten year period from 1988 through 1998 and the three year period from 1997 through the great Jubilee Year of 2000.

The Virgin Mary discloses to Fr. Stefano Gobbi that the ten year period has great significance for mankind because these years will witness what She had predicted at Fatima in 1917.

Our Lady also said that Her Immaculate Heart will have already triumphed "by the great Jubilee Year of 2000." What does this mean? She speaks of a Second Pentecost. What does this mean?

She speaks of the Second Coming and a Final Coming, and the Reign of Christ. What does this mean?

Our Lady said to Fr. Gobbi that we will understand why the last three years before the year 2000 justify our seeking refuge in Her Immaculate Heart if we but listen to Her words. What can be facing mankind that would justify such dire words?

The Holy Father, Pope John Paul II, speaks of a "new spring-time" for the Church and asks for a very special spiritual preparation during the years 1997 through 1999 for the year 2000 in his Apostolic Letter *Tertio Millenio Adveniente*. He discusses the hope for mankind in his book *Crossing The Threshold of Hope*.

It would seem that every Catholic would be curious to know in detail the messages of Our Lady who has come as a prophet to warn us of our transgressions and that we are all at risk, and to read Her words of the merciful love available to us *if we act now.* It also seems that the Holy Father sees, with the Blessed Virgin, that great experiences are looming on the horizon in the year 2000 — for us and the Church. This book addresses the question — what does this all mean for us? By citing specific paragraphs (all are words of Our Lady) from Fr. Gobbi's book *To The Priests — Our Lady's Beloved Sons* and quoting some of the Holy Father's thoughts on the year 2000, some of these questions might at least be partially answered.

All bold and italic type is used by the author for emphasis. All parenthetical comments used after Our Lady's words are by the author.

CHAPTER 1

The End of an Era

There is much speculation among many Christians concerning what might happen in the world in the year 2000. Some think that possibly even before that year there will come dire world-wide conditions which will be life threatening to a large part of humanity; conditions such as war, famine, earthquakes, devastating weather and diseases, and the possible cosequences of global warming. There has always been an element of the doomsday crowd that predicts the end of the world on such and such a day and at such and such a time. The daily news has carried the sad incidents where people have taken their own lives so they could travel on mysterious space ships to avoid the death of this planet earth. Other bizarre schemes have been publicized and, of course, nothing has happened and the end of the world has not come.

There is reason to believe, however, that we are approaching the end of a period of time, an end of this era, according to the words published by the Marian Movement of Priests (MMP) in the book titled *To The Priests — Our Lady's Beloved Sons*. According to an Italian priest named Father Stefano Gobbi, he has received words spoken as interior locutions (messages) from the Blessed Virgin Mary since 1973 in which She says we are coming to the *end of an era* which will have great significance for mankind, a time of great suffering, chaos, and confusion. She uses the terms: Purification, Tribulation, and Chastisement.

Of current interest among the clergy, religious, and lay members of the MMP are the predictions and prophecies concerning the years preceding the year 2000, prophecies allegedly from the Mother of God Herself. Although the Church teaches that we should never assign specific dates and times to future events that are part of prophecy, certain events have been predicted in a general sense and many of these have come to pass as predicted, for example, those prophesied by Our Lady in Fatima, Portugal in 1917. It does not seem, therefore, that it was coincidence that while on pilgrimage to Fatima, Portugal in 1973, Fr. Gobbi received his first locutions from Our Lady asking him to begin the Marian Movement of Priests.

In this book, from the 1,034 pages of locutions to Fr. Gobbi, we will narrow down to those specific locutions which refer to the period of 1988 to 1998, the years from 1998 to the year 2000, and those which describe the Tribulation and the problems within the Church. I have selected specific paragraphs which will be cited by number for the convenience of the readers who possess a copy of *To The Priests — Our Lady's Beloved Sons*.

Only once in all of Her locutions to Fr. Gobbi does Mary refer to the final judgement (end of the world) — in par. 166e. Otherwise, She speaks of *the end of the times* or *the end of this era*. What does Mary say about the ten years and the year 2000? We will attempt to answer that question in the following pages as Mary clearly tells us that before the final judgement we will face a "judgement in miniature" and a chastisement to cleanse and save humanity from its evil path.

Credibility of: *To The Priests – Our Lady's Beloved Sons*

The 1997 Supplement Edition of Fr. Gobbi's book carries the Imprimatur of Cardinal Bernardino Echeverria Ruiz, OFM, Archbishop Emeritus of Guayaquil and Apostolic Administrator of Ibarra, dated Feb. 2, 1998. This Imprimatur includes the words "I consider it a privilege, not only to be able to give the Imprimatur to this edition of the book *To The Priests — Our Lady's Beloved Sons*, but also to take this opportunity to recommend the reading of these messages. They will contribute to the spread of devotion to Our Lady."

This book also contains the Imprimatur of Donald W. Montrose, D.D., Bishop of Stockton, dated Feb. 2, 1998, in which he states, "There is nothing contrary to faith and morals in this manuscript."

The author strongly recommends that the reader read the 17th Edition of *To The Priests...* and in particular the Notes From The Spiritual Director in the front part of the book to better understand the signs of the times in which we are living and the crisis of faith as foretold by Our Lady in Fatima in 1917.

It is left to the conscience and free will of the reader to read and believe or to read and reject the admonitions, warnings, and words of encourgement of Our Lady as She speaks of these "end times." Under Catholic Church canon law we are free to accept or reject locutions and apparitions. We are permitted to read and believe so long as they have not been condemned by the Church.

It is reasonable to assume that Fr. Gobbi and his spiritual director have accurately reflected Our Lady's words in the book, *To The Priests...*, considering their devotion to Our Lady and to the Marian Movement of Priests. They have been totally dedicated to propagating Her words in spite of non-acceptance by some members of the clergy who would spare them no criticism if given the opportunity to find fault with the book.

CHAPTER 2

Certain Significant Periods of Time

Considerable attention has recently been given to the meaning and impact of the words of Our Lady as She spoke of the ten year period of 1988 to 1998, and of the Great Jubilee Year of Two Thousand. It seems highly significant that Our Lady specifies that "fullness of time... beginning with La Salette all the way to my most recent and present apparitions." This fullness of time includes Her apparitions at Lourdes, Fatima and Akita and other apparitions approved by the Church, most of which foretell serious consequences for a very sinful world. Our Lady says that in this period of ten years the purification will come to its completion, the tribulation will come to its completion, the Anti-Christ will become manifest, and the spread of apostasy will increase. She said all the events foretold by Her will take place and all the secrets revealed to visionaries will come to pass in this ten year period. It would seem we would all be curious about these events and secrets — how do they apply to us as individuals?; how do we cope with them?; is there real hope for us?; what should we do?; what can we do?; is there a refuge for us sinful but repentant creatures?

A Period of Ten Years and The Great Jubilee Year of Two-Thousand (Par. 389)

(389c) On September18, 1988 in Lourdes, France at the Cenacle with priests and the faithful of the MMP, Our Lady said, "On this day I am asking you to consecrate to me all of the time that still separates you from the end of this century of yours. It is a period of ten years. These are ten very important years. These are ten very decisive years. I am asking you to spend them with me because you are entering into the final period of the Second Advent, which will lead you to the triumph of My Immaculate Heart in the glorious coming of My Son Jesus."

(389d) "In this period of ten years there will come to completion that fullness of time which was pointed out to you by me, beginning with La Salette all the way to my most recent and present apparitions." (For a description of the "fullness of time" referred to here, see the end of par. 389h below).

(389e) "In this period of ten years there will come to its culmination that purification which, for a number of years now, you have been living through and therefore the sufferings will become greater for all."

(389f) "In this period of ten years there will come to completion the time of the great tribulation, which has been foretold to you in Holy Scripture, before the second coming of Jesus."

(389g) "In this period of ten years the mystery of iniquity (Anti-Christ), prepared for by the ever increasing spread of apostasy, will become manifest."

(389h) "In this period of ten years all the secrets which I have revealed to some of my children will come to pass and all the events which have been foretold you by me will take place."

Explanation of *That Fullness of Time* and *Ominous Signs of Warning*

These words refer to the second coming of Christ with the "new heavens and a new earth" after the great trial. In par. 389f above the completion of the great tribulation will have taken place before the second coming of Jesus. The following paragraphs describe the conditions, events, sufferings, the Church, and Mary's role during this period of ten years, the period of the great tribulation. These are the alleged words of Our Lady. They are very sad and frightening words, but prophets do not generally speak words of joy and happiness — they most often are words of warning and the consequences.

It is downright misleading, however, to characterize these words as "doom and gloom" messages when, in fact, they are words of warning that gush from the Divine Mercy of God for our own salvation. God could just as easily have punished Sodom and Gomorrah without having warned the people with the warning of the prophets. He chose to act as the Merciful Father as He does today. Those who almost hysterically pooh-pooh the prophetic words of Mary in Her locutions and apparitions as words of doom and gloom may be minimizing the sinful conditions of this world and might be inadvertantly encouraging a continuance of the abominable behavior of mankind as revealed in the following words of Our Lady.

Again, we emphasize — YES — Jesus loves us as we are. The warnings from Our Lady are to wake up those who might be aware of His love but seem to have forgotten about His justice — and are now encouraged by Our Lady to change immediately and be repentent because the chastisement is on its way to purify a world that "is a thousand times worse than at the time of the flood" (Our Lady to Fr. Gobbi). These are not words of doom and gloom but are words from LOVE and MERCY itself — Our Lady, Queen of Mercy; words of mercy and hope from our Heavenly Father:

(485d) "These signs are clearly indicated in the Gospels, in the letters of Saint Peter and Saint Paul, and they are becoming a reality during these years."

(485e) "The first sign is the spread of errors which lead to the loss of faith and to apostasy. These errors are being propagated by false teachers, by renowned theologians who are no longer teaching the truths of the Gospel, but pernicious heresies based on errors and on human reasonings... It is because of these errors that the true faith is being lost and that the great apostasy is spreading everywhere." (Apostasy means the loss of faith). See Mt 24, 4-5;2 Thes 2-3; 2 Pt 2, 1-3.

(485f) "The second sign is the outbreak of wars and fratracidal struggles... while natural catastrophes, such as epidemics, famines, floods and earthquakes, become more and more frequent." See Mt 24, 6-8. 12-13.

(485l) "The third sign is the bloody persecution of those who remain faithful to Jesus and his Gospel and who stand fast in the true faith..." See Mt 24, 9-10...14.

(485o) "The fourth sign is the horrible sacrilege, perpetrated by him who sets himself against Christ, that is, the Anti-Christ. He will enter into the holy temple of God and will sit on his throne, and have himself adored as God." See 2 Thes 2, 4, 9 and Mt 24, 15 "In this abolition of the daily sacrifice (the Holy Mass) consists the horrible sacrilege accomplished by the Anti-Christ..."

(485v) "The fifth sign consists in extraordinary phenomena, which occur in the skies."

(485x) "The miracle of the sun, which took place at Fatima during my last apparition, is intended to point out to you that you are now entering into the times when those events will take place, events which will prepare for the return of Jesus in glory (Second Coming)."

(485y) "And then the sign of the Son of man will appear in heaven. All the tribes of the earth will mourn, and men will see the Son of Man coming upon the clouds of heaven, with great power and splendor." See Mt24, 30.

(485A) "The year which is coming to a close (1992), and that which is beginning, form part of the great tribulation, during which the apostasy is spreading, the wars are multiplying, natural catastrophes are occurring in many places, persecutions are intensifying, the announcement of the Gospel is being brought to all nations, extraordinary phenomena are occurring in the sky, and the moment of the full manifestation of the Anti-Christ is drawing ever nearer."

CHAPTER 3

Further Details of the Tribulation Period – Our Lady's Predictions at Fatima in 1917, Their Fulfillment, and Critical Problems in the Church

For those of you who have not been keeping abreast of the deterioration of conditions within the Church, you might react with numbness when you now read what Our Lady describes:

(473a) "Beloved children, today you are observing the 75th anniversary of my first apparition, which took place at Fatima in the Cova da Iria, on the 13th of May, 1917..."

(473b) "At that time I predicted the times of the loss of the true faith and the apostasy which would spread throughout every part of the Church. You are living in the times of which I foretold.

(473c) "At that time I predicted the times of the war and of the persecution of the Church and the Holy Father, because of the spread of theoretical atheism and of the rebellion of humanity against God and His law."

(473d) "At that time I predicted the chastisement and that, in the end, my Immaculate Heart would have its triumph."

(464c) "The activity of my Adversary (Satan) to extend his reign over all humanity, will become stronger. Thus evil and sin, violence and hatred, perversion and unbelief will increase everywhere. Wars will spread..."

(464e) "Even in the Church, the darkness will descend more densely yet, and will succeed in enveloping everything. Errors will spread much more and many will wander away from the true faith. Apostasy will spread like an epidemic and pastors will be stricken by it along with the flocks entrusted to them. In every part of the earth, the Church, this poor agonizing and crucified daughter of mine, will have much to suffer."

(464f) "The contestation directed against the Pope will become stronger; theologians, bishops, priests and laity will openly oppose his Magisterium. My Pope will feel himself more and more alone, as he is abandoned, criticized, and ridiculed by many."

(442h) "You have entered into the conclusive period of the great tribulation, and the hour of the great trial of which I have been foretelling you for so many years, has now arrived for you. It is a trial so great and painful, that you cannot even imagine it, but it is necessary for the Church and for all humanity, in order that the new era, the new world, and the reconciliation of humanity with their Lord, may come upon you."

(332f) **"Because this humanity has not accepted my repeated call to conversion, to repentance, and to a return to God, there is about to fall upon it the greatest chastisement which the history of mankind has ever known. It is a chastisement much greater than that of the flood. Fire will fall from heaven and a great part of humanity will be destroyed."**

(332g) "The Church of Jesus is wounded with the pernicious plague of infidelity and apostasy. In appearance everything remains calm and it seems that all is going well. **In reality, she is being pervaded with an overwhelming lack of faith which is spreading the great apostasy everywhere.** *Many bishops, priests, religious and faithful no longer believe and have already lost the true faith in Jesus and in his Gospel. For this reason the Church must be purified with persecution and with blood."*

(332h) "There has entered into the Church disunity, division, strife and antagonism. The forces of atheism and Masonry, having infiltrated it, are on the point of breaking up its interior unity and of darkening the splendor of its sanctity. **These are the times foretold by me, when cardinals will be set against cardinals, bishops against bishops, and priests against priests and the flock of Christ will be torn to pieces by rapacious wolves who have found their way in under the clothing of defenseless and meek lambs.** *Among them there are even some who occupy posts of great responsibility and, by means of them, Satan has succeeded in entering and in operating at the very summit of the Church. Bishops and priests of the holy Church of God, how great is your responsibility!*

The Lord is about to demand of you an account of how you have administered his vineyard. Repent, seek pardon, make amends, and above all, be once again faithful to the task which has been entrusted to you."

(332i) "Sin is being committed more and more. It is no longer acknowledged as an evil. It is sought out. It is consciously willed and it is no longer confessed. Impurity and lewdness cover the homes built by your rebellion."

(332j) "This is the reason my heart is bleeding; because of the obstinate disbelief and the hardness of your hearts."

(332k) "My heart is bleeding to see you so closed and insensitive to my sorrowful motherly admonition."

(3321) "My heart is bleeding because I see your roads even now smeared with blood, while you live in an obstinate unconsciousness of that which awaits you."

CHAPTER 4

The Last Secret of Fatima, Chastisement and the Anti-Christ

One of the greatest controversies in the Church concerning the revelations at Fatima revolves around the fact that the third secret given at Fatima in 1917 was to have been revealed publicly in 1960 but has not been made know to this date. Now Our Lady here refers to that secret and tells us we will know that secret from the very occurrences that take place in our world. The time she describes will be a time of great penance and suffering, and clearly refers to the failures of leadership within the Church and a growth in heresy and apostasy, and the activity of the Anti-Christ:

(425f) "I am coming down from heaven so that the final secrets may be revealed to you and that I may be able to prepare you for what, as of now, you must live through, for the purification of the earth.

(425g) "My third secret, which I revealed here (in Fatima) to three little children to whom I appeared and which up to the present has not yet been revealed to you, will be made manifest to all by the very occurrence of the events."

(425h) *"The Church will know the hour of its greatest apostasy. The man of iniquity (the Anti-Christ) will penetrate into its interior and will sit in the very Temple of God, while the little remnant which will remain faithful will be subjected to the greatest trials and persecutions.*

(425j) *"Humanity will live through the moment of its greatest chastisement* **and thus will be made ready to receive the Lord Jesus who will return in glory.**

(112h) "Where today is there a place where sin does not exist? Even those houses consecrated to the worship of God are profaned by the sins that are committed in them. It is the persons who are consecrated, the very priests and religious, who have lost even the sense of sin. Some of them, in their thoughts, their words, and their way of life sacrilegiously allow themselves to be led by Satan."

(112l) *"Satan has now pitched his tents even among the ministers of the sanctuary and has brought the abomination of desolation into the holy Temple."*

(501g) "In this very country (Akita, Japan) I have given you an extraordinary sign, causing copious tears to fall more than a hundred times from the eyes of one of my statues, in which I am represented as the Sorrowful Mother beneath the Cross of my Son, Jesus. And I have given you *three messages to warn you of the great dangers into which you are running."*

(501h) *"I now announce to you that the time of the great trial has come, because during these years all that I foretold to you will come to pass. The apostasy and the great schism in the Church is on the point of taking place and the great chastisement, about which I foretold you in this place, is now at the very doors. Fire will come down from heaven and a great part of humanity will be destroyed. Those who survive will envy the dead, because everywhere there will be desolation, death and ruin."*

(501i) "And so once again... you must tell all that *the hour of the chastisement has come and that, in order to be protected and saved, they must all enter right away into the safe refuge of my Immaculate Heart."*

(507e) *"During these years, you will see the great chastisement,* with which the justice of God will purify this world, which has become a thousand times worse than at the time of the flood, and so very possessed by evil spirits."

(509e) "Masonry, with its diabolical power, has set up its center in the very heart of the Church, where the Vicar of my Son Jesus resides, and from there it is spreading its evil influence to every part of the world. And now the Church will once again be betrayed by its own; it will be cruelly persecuted and led to the gibbet."

(527h) *"My Pope is becoming more and more isolated, mocked, criticized and abandoned. Many from among the bishops and the priests are going along the road of disloyalty and are fading away like lights which are now burnt out. Many voracious wolves, in sheep's clothing, are entering in to inflict slaughter on the sheepfold of my Son, Jesus."*

(542f) "... And how much blood flows down again from the weeping eyes of your heavenly mother! It is the blood of children killed in the wombs of their mothers. It is the blood poured out by all the victims of violence and hatred, of fratricidal struggles and wars and again copious tears flow down from my motherly eyes in the face of humanity which bears within itself the reason for its own condemnation."

(542h) "...And yet these very grave signs, which I am giving you today, are neither accepted nor given credence, but on the contrary are openly opposed and rejected..."

(542j) "...I see your roads smeared with tears and blood. Thus this world will be purified by divine justice; this world which has touched the bottom of perversion and of rebellion against its God who, for your salvation, is being immolated and put to death on the Cross."

(548i) "I have also revealed to you the subtle and diabolical snares set for you by Masonry, which entered into the interior of the Church and has established the center of its power there where Jesus has established the center and the foundation of her unity. Do not be disturbed because this forms part of the mystery of iniquity which the Church has known from her very birth. In fact, *Satan — who drove Judas, one of the twelve, to become the traitor — has entered even into the Apostolic College.*"

(548j) *"In these times of yours, the mystery of iniquity (Anti-Christ) is on the point of manifesting itself in all its terrible power."*

The preceding paragraphs have provided a comprehensive description of the tribulation time, the time we are now living in — a time before the chastisement — and, therefore, the most significant time of preparation and reparation in the history of mankind as it concerns our salvation and the crossing of the threshold of hope into a new era of peace, love, and joy for the surviving remnant:

(587n) "During this year (1997), in which you are beginning the spiritual preparation for the Great Jubilee (of two thousand), I invite you to follow me along the way of a deeper understanding of the mystery of Jesus Christ, true God and King of eternal glory."

(586j) "Make reparation for the sins of this poor humanity which finds itself completely under the power of my Adversary... The law of the Lord is being completely subverted and even the gravest moral disorders are being legitimized... As of now this poor humanity has touched the bottom of its misery. It can no longer succeed in recovering if a great act of mercy does not raise it up." (This reveals the importance of the Divine Mercy devotions, sacraments, Mass, and conversion.)

(586m) "Make reparation for the infidelities of so many sons of the Church... Errors are being spread, taught and followed... Who will remain firm in the faith, in Jesus, and his Church?"

Our Lady begs us for a complete conversion during the three years preceding the year 2000. We are to make reparation and remain firm in the faith. The average Catholic is totally unaware, at this very moment, of these conditions in the Church and the requests She makes of *us for our own good!*

CHAPTER 5

The Remnant and the Triumph of Mary's Immaculate Heart

Our Lady calls for those who will make up the remnant to be instrumental in the triumph of Her Immaculate Heart, which is simply the glorious Reign of Jesus on earth in the hearts and souls of the faithful remnant.

(586r) *"Never, as in these three years (1997-1999) which separate you from the great Jubilee, will it become clear to the Church and to humanity, in an increasingly powerful way, how my Immaculate Heart will be your safe refuge."*

(558h) "My plan is to point out to all my children the way of faith and of hope, of love, and of purity, of goodness and of holiness. Thus, in the garden of my Immaculate Heart, *I am preparing the little remnant who,* in the midst of the tempestuous waves of the apostasy and the perversion, *will remain faithful to Christ, to the Gospel, and to the Church."*

(558i) *"And it will be with this little flock,* guarded in the Immaculate Heart of your heavenly Mother, **that Jesus will bring about his glorious reign in the world."** (The Second Advent — The Second Coming)

On December 5th, 1994 in Mexico City, at the Shrine of Our Lady of Guadalupe, Our Lady told Fr. Gobbi. *"By the great*

Jubilee Year of Two Thousand, there will take place the triumph of my Immaculate Heart of which I foretold you at Fatima, and this will come to pass with the return of Jesus in glory to establish his reign in the world. Then you will be able to see with your own eyes the new heavens and the new earth."

Two Questions

Two questions are raised in Our Lady's words that need to be answered if we are to fully understand and know what to expect concerning the great Jubilee Year of two thousand. These questions are 1) *what does Our Lady mean by the "Triumph of her Immaculate Heart?"* and 2) *what does She mean by "the return of Jesus in glory to establish his reign in the world?"*

The Triumph of Her Immaculate Heart

For the answer to this question we must look to Her words given to Fr. Gobbi in 1973. The triumph of Her Immaculate Heart is always discussed by Her in the context of victory over Satan, accomplished with Her cohort of the clergy, religious, and laity who are loyal to Her Son, Jesus, the Holy Father, to the Magisterium, and to Her, — together with the return of Jesus for His Glorious Reign:

(29e) "I have chosen you and prepared you for the triumph of my Immaculate Heart in the world, and *these are the years when I will bring my plan to completion."*

(29f) "It will be a cause of amazement even to the angels of God; a joy to the saints in heaven; a consolation and great comfort for all the just on earth. *Mercy and salvation* for a great number of my straying children; a severe and definitive condemnation of Satan and his many followers."

(29g) "In fact at the very moment when Satan will be enthroned as lord of the world and will think himself now the sure victor, I myself will snatch the prey from his hands. In a trice he will find himself empty-handed and in the end the victory will be exclusively my Son's and mine. *This will be the triumph of my Immaculate Heart in the world.*"

(116p) ***"The triumph of the Heart of the Mother is won in the souls and the lives of her faithful children."***

(116q) "In them it is good which triumphs at the very moment when evil is spreading everywhere. While sin tries to pervade everything, the grace and the love of God triumph in them; if error succeeds more and more in corrupting minds, they bear witness to the truth."

(116r) "If division tears the Church, they love her and live for her unity; if the Vicar of my Son is more and more left alone and abandoned, they draw close to him with greater love to become his constant comfort and defense."

The demands on those who desire to be a faithful member of THE REMNANT are the makings of saints. No one should be lulled into thinking that a wimpish approach to living the teachings of the authentic Catholic Church will qualify one to be a real soldier in this select group. Read again par. 116r, immediately above. Can we fully realize what it can mean to be the constant defense of the Holy Father? This will require a brave proclaiming of your faith in every kind of attack on the Church or its teachings as manifested in the entertainment world, the local and national newspapers, or in the work place. You might be required to defend the Faith within your own family. Jesus said that in these times mother will turn against daughter, and daughter against mother, etc. We will need to fight for the unity within the Church. We can expect this will alienate us from friends who are not faithful but consider themselves to be believing Catholics. The remnant will bear witness to the truth — and this might cost the martyrdom of many. The remnant will be those called and chosen as well! But they will EARN IT!

CHAPTER 6

Mercy and Salvation with a Second Pentecost

Notice in par. 29g above, that "MERCY and SALVATION for a great number" is an integral characteristic of Our Lady's triumph. Through Her appeal for mercy to Her Son, the Holy Spirit will enlighten mankind in its folly and complacency. The Holy Spirit will reinvigorate the faithful to conversion. Those who cooperate with the grace of God will become the remnant.

(521i) "A new fire will come down from heaven and will purify all humanity, which has become pagan. It will be like a judgement in miniature and each one will see himself in the light of the very truth of God." (We will know ourselves as God knows us in all our weakness.)

(521j) "Thus sinners will come back to grace and holiness; the straying, to the road of righteousness; those far away, to the house of the Father; the sick, to complete healing; and the proud, the impure; the wicked collaborators with Satan will be defeated and condemned forever."

(521k) *Then my Heart-of-a-Mother will have its triumph over all humanity, which will return to a new marriage of love and of life with its Heavenly Father."*

(562i,j) "I am the Mother of Love and of Mercy. At the moment when the world will be set free from the Evil One and the earth purified by the painful trial which, in many ways, has already been foretold to you, my Immaculate Heart will be the place where *all will see fulfilled the greatest prodigy of Divine Mercy.*"

(562k) *"Thus the Holy Spirit will pour out upon the world his Second Pentecost of grace and fire, to prepare the Church and humanity for the return of Jesus in the splendor of his divine glory to make all things new."*

CHAPTER 7

The Reign of Jesus
in the Second Coming

The return of Jesus in glory to "establish his reign in the world" presents the second question, i.e., what does this mean?Will Jesus walk the earth again in His glorified body?; what form will His reign take? It seems He will reign through the converted hearts of those who *received His mercy and survived the chastisement.* Apparently He will appear to man in His glorified body but will not "live" on the earth during His new reign except in the hearts of His flock. EACH ONE will share the experience Peter, James, and John had at the Ascension. If each one on earth is to share this experience of the three apostles, then it appears evident that this will take place only after the chastisement and the purification of the earth. That surviving remnant will be in the state of grace, worthy of such an experience, and it will happen to each one on earth who is alive at that period of the reign of Christ, having been brought about by the action of the Second Pentecost:

(597j) "When Jesus will return in his divine glory and appear to all humanity, *each one* will be called to undergo the same experience as Peter, James, and John underwent on Mount Tabor, because Jesus will manifest himself in his splendor, and his humanity will be completely transfigured in the most brilliant light of his divinity."

(597k) "Then the whole universe will proclaim Jesus Christ as the Son of God, the perfect Image of the Father, the Word made man, the one and only Savior, He through whom all things have been made and who has the power to subject all things to Himself. Jesus will bring his glorious kingdom into the world, and it will be a kingdom of holiness and grace, a kingdom of justice and of peace." (His kingdom will reign in our hearts when we become His image on earth).

(505c) *"The glorious reign of Christ will be above all established in hearts and souls.* This is the most precious part of the divine royalty of Jesus."

(505d) *"... Those hearts renewed by Love and those souls sanctified by grace form then the most precious part of the divine royalty of Jesus."*

(505e) "The glorious reign of Christ will correspond to a general flowering of holiness and purity, of love and justice, of joy and peace. For the hearts of men will be transformed by the powerful force of the Holy Spirit, *Who will pour Himself out upon them through the miracle of his Second Pentecost."*

(505f) "And souls will be enlightened by the presence of the Most Holy Trinity, who will produce in them an extraordinary unfolding of all the virtues."

Conformance to the Will of God

(505g) "...The glorious reign of Christ will coincide, then, with the the perfect accomplishment of the will of God on the part of everyone of his creatures, *in such a way that, as it is in heaven, so it will be on earth."*

(505i) "The glorious reign of Christ will be established after the complete defeat of Satan and all the spirits of evil, and the destruction of Satan's diabolical power. Thus he will be bound and cast into hell, and the gates of the abyss will be shut so that he can no longer get out to harm the world. And Christ will reign in the world."

The Eucharistic Reign of Christ

(505j) *"The glorious reign of Christ will coincide with the triumph of the eucharistic reign of Jesus,* because in a purified and sanctified world, completely renewed by Love, Jesus will be made manifest above all in the mystery of his eucharistic presence."

(505k) "The Eucharist will be the source from which will burst forth all his divine power, and it will become the new sun which will shed its bright rays in hearts and souls, and then in the life of individuals, families, and nations, *making of all one single flock, docile and meek, whose sole Shepherd will be Jesus."*

The Virgin Mary, Fr. Gobbi and the Year 2000

CHAPTER 8

The Holy Father and the Great Jubilee Year of Two Thousand

The Holy Father has designated 1997, 1998, and 1999 as three years of preparation for the Jubilee Year of 2000. Our Lady told Fr. Gobbi on December 31, 1996, "This special preparation which the Pope is urging on you through his apostolic letter, *Tertio Millenio Adveniente*, is to make you understand that *this date is important for the Church and all humanity. This date should be particularly significant for you because I have previously announced to you, for that date (2000), the triumph of My Immaculate Heart in the world." (see par. 586d)*

(586h) "Pray to obtain the great gift of the Second Pentecost, implored and awaited by you. It will be the Holy Spirit who will give to the world his full and perfect witness to Jesus."

(586i) "Jesus Christ must be welcomed, loved, adored and followed by all humanity as your one and only Redeemer and Savior. The Holy Spirit will open the minds and hearts of all to receive the light of the truth. And thus there will be one single flock under one single Shepherd."

(586r) *"Never as in these final three years which separate you from the great Jubilee, will it become clear to the Church and to humanity, in an increasingly powerful way, how my Immaculate Heart will be your safe refuge."*

It should be apparent from the paragraph 586r above, that conditions for these three years will be such as to draw us to the refuge of the Immaculate Heart of Mary. Those conditions are descibed in detail in the section above titled "A Period of Ten Years." *This period includes the time of the purification, and the time of the tribulation, and certainly appears to include the time of the chastisement within this period or perhaps sometime before the year 2000 unless God cancels the chastisement due to the conversion of the world.*

How should we interpret Our Lady's words in which She describes the period of ten years which include the three years of preparation leading up to the Jubilee year of 2000? Are we to understand that only the remnant of faithful will experience the New Era? Does this remnant include those who received the great Mercy which is to come through the enlightenment of many by the Holy Spirit in the Second Pentecost? It seems that this is so because Our Lady speaks of a number of postponements of the chastisement that would permit an increase in the number of conversions due to the actions of the Holy Spirit and the subsequent awakening of the conscience of humanity. When She says Satan will be defeated and bound in the abyss, it includes the souls who rejected God during the tribulation and refused to convert in spite of the warnings and help of the Holy Spirit at the time of the Warning or Enlightenment.

We need to pray that all will be touched by God's grace and come to conversion, but OurLady herself says many will prefer Satan to Jesus and seek damnation at the time of the great trial. They will refuse to cooperate with the special grace and mercy available during these years immediately before the time of the actual chastisement, especially the years immediately preceding the years of 1999 and 2000.

CHAPTER 9

Things Can Be Changed

It seems Our Lady takes great pains to inform us that 1) *things can change through penance, prayer, and suffering — including the time of the chastisement itself,* and 2) *in spite of Her own predictions for the human race — we are not to fear and we are not to be anxious* because the Lord will inundate the world with His Merciful Love through means of the Warning or Enlightenment or the Illunination, and the Second Pentecost for all mankind, both of which being a manifestation of His Mercy. She indicated to Fr. Gobbi a number of times that the culmination of *the chastisement has been postponed* due to prayers of the faithful and Her intercession with Her Son. It is not clear from Fr. Gobbi's book when the chastisement will culminate even though She foretells the terrible suffering for mankind during the ten year period. *She clearly says that conditions can change because of prayer, fasting, and repentence.* Mary tells us that Mercy is for all who seek it and the Second Pentecost is for all who will live the Gospels and make up the remnant — those who reform their lives, and the just who have remained faithful during the great Apostasy. The remnant will be the one single flock under the one single Shepherd:

(142g) "During this year (1977) which is about to end, *I have been able to hold off the chastisement* because of prayers and sufferings of many of my children. Your *yes* has enabled me to add strength to my action of maternal intercession on your behalf."

(184g) ***"Everything can still be changed for you, my children;*** *listen to my voice and unite yourselves through prayer with the unceasing intercession of your heavenly Mother"*

(195b) "My plan does not correspond with yours, and my ways are not yours. *You will be able to understand my plan and walk in my way, only if you have a pure heart."*

(216e) *"At the hour when all will seem lost, all will be saved* through the merciful love of the Father, which will be made visible through the greatest manifestation of the Eucharistic Heart of Jesus."

For those who anxiously "look forward" to the chastisement of the world and even seem disappointed that it has not yet come, the following words of Mary offer sound guidance as to what our attitude shoud be concerning any postponement of that dreadful time:

(316c) "Do not allow yourselves to be seduced by those *who point to years and days, as though they wanted to impose a time-table* on the infinite mercy of the divine Heart of my Son, Jesus."

(113p) *"Live then in the serenity of spirit and without fear,* even in the midst of the anxieties and threats of your time."

(113q) "And so I say again: *do not be always peering into the future to see what is going to happen.* Live only the present moment with trust and complete abandonment in this heart of mine."

(441i) *"...do not let yourselves be seized by fear or discouragement. Have great confidence* in the powerful work of intercession and mediation of your heavenly Mother."

(473k) *"The more this motherly triumph comes about* in the hearts and souls of my children in ever increasing numbers, *the more the chastisement is put off by you* and the more Jesus can pour out upon the world the torrents of His Divine Mercy."
(The more souls are consecrated to Our Lady's Immaculate Heart and live that consecration, the more Mary can postpone the chastisement.) (1992)

(553g) "How many times have I already intervened *in order to set back further and further in time the beginning of the great trial,* for the purification of this poor humanity, now possessed and dominated by the Spirits of Evil." (1995)

(576f) "...I gather in the chalice of my Immaculate Heart all your sufferings, the great sorrows of all humanity in the time of its great tribulation and *I present them to Jesus as a sign of reparation for all the sins* which are committed each day in the world." (1996)

(576g) "And thus *I have again succeeded in postponing the time of the chastisement* decreed by Divine Justice for a humanity which has become worse than at the time of the flood." (1996)

(205g) *"Don't be curious to know what is waiting for you,* but at each moment live in perfect love..."

(205h) "Your mission is sublime, and you must not let it come to a stop through weakness or human discouragement."

The task of all is to live a eucharistic life while complying with God's laws, confessing our sins, converting our ways, and praying for oursleves and others, especially the clergy and religious, as Mary requested in Fatima. Our prime concern now is the salvation of our own soul and the souls of "those for whom no one prays." We truly are a large component of God's plan of salvation when we pray for others and make reparation for sin.

Our particular judgement ought not be the time when we discover we failed in that Catholic responsibility. God's ways are not our ways. Place the future in His hands, while we live the eucharistic life in the present.

CHAPTER 10

Why the Postponement
of the Chastisement?

What would be the heavenly purpose of postponing the great trial or the chastisement if it were not for the possibility of gaining additional souls during the preparation for the Reign of Jesus? Let us remember that Our Lady has said that during this trial a great part of humanity would die, and apparently many will die in an instant. It must be part of Her plan to delay this terrible period in order to have the extra time to save as many souls as possible before the Divine Justice falls upon us. *Thus, the postponement is actually an act of Merciful Love.*

From the time of the Warning (or enlightenment or illumination) to the time of the actual chastisement millions upon millions can be saved who would have otherwise been lost before their conversion. Our Lady says also that She will not permit harm to come to those consecrated to Her. What does this mean? Are they to be brought through the trial without bodily harm? The answer is no, this is not what She means when She speaks of Her protection for souls consecrated to Her. In paragraph 236c and par. 236d Our Lady says, "You are thus signed with the seal of my love, which distinguishes you from those who have allowed themselves to be seduced by the Beast and bear his imprinted blasphemous number (666). The Dragon (Satan) and the Beast (Anti-Christ and Masonry) can do nothing against those who have been signed by my seal." In par. 236d Our Lady clarifies that "the Star of the Abyss (Satan) will persecute all those who are signed with my seal, *but nothing will be able to harm the souls* upon whom I myself have impressed my image. *By the blood which many of them will shed,* divine justice will be appeased and the time of my victory will be hastened..."

So we see that Mary's protection is primarily the salvation of the souls of those consecrated to Her, many of whom will die as martyrs who had been marked with Her mark of salvation.

A New Era — The End Times —
The Second Advent — The Day of The Lord

After the Great Trial (purification, tribulation and chastisement) Our Lady foretells the end of this period of time in which we are now living, an end of an era which She refers to as THE END TIMES. Then she foretells of a new era on earth, the New Times:

(424g) "A little while yet and the door of this immense sepulchre in which lies all humanity, will be opened. *Jesus Christ,* surrounded by the choir of Angels — on the clouds of heaven prostrate at his feet to form a royal throne — in the splendor of his divinity, *will return to bring humanity to a new life, souls to grace and love, the Church to its highest summit of sanctity, and He will thus restore in the world his reign of glory.*" (spoken in 1990)

(234h) "The darkness will be conquered by a light which will cover the whole world; the cold of hatred, by the fire of love; the great rebellion against God, by a universal return to his merciful fatherly love."

(435b) "I reveal my secret. Today I announce to you that *there is about to be born the new Church of Light,* which my Son is forming for Himself in every part of the earth, so that it will be ready to receive him with faith and with joy, *in the proximate moment of his second coming.*"

(435c) *"The glorious reign of Christ, which will be established in the world, is close at hand. This is his return in glory. This is his glorious return to establish his reign in your midst and to bring all humanity, redeemed by his Most Precious Blood, back to the state of his terrestrial paradise..."*

(435d) "That which is being prepared is so great that its equal has never existed since the creation of the world..."

(435e) "I reveal my secret only to the hearts of the little, the simple, and the poor because it is being accepted and believed by them..."

(435f) *"With a small number of these children,* the Lord will soon restore on earth his glorious reign of love, of holiness and of peace." (This "small number of children" apparently refers to the remnant. This is an ominous prediction for the world but good news for the faithful.)

(436e) "In the hour of the great trial, paradise will be joined to earth, until the moment when the luminous door will be opened to cause to descend upon the world the glorious presence of Christ Who will restore his reign..."

(186x) "Therefore, I say to you: soon the desert will blossom and *all creation will become again that marvellous garden,* created for man to reflect in a perfect manner the greatest glory of God."

The Virgin Mary, Fr. Gobbi and the Year 2000

CHAPTER 11

The Holy Father,
the Threshold of Hope

The Holy Father, Pope John Paul II, seems also to allude to a special time for the Jubilee Year of 2000 in his book *Crossing the Threshold of Hope*. He points to the period of time beginning in the third millenium and his preparatory period of 1997 through 1999 as a critical time to study the Faith as it is established in the Father, Son, and Holy Spirit with the heroic and redemptive love of the Blessed Virgin Mary. (See his apostolic letter *Tertio Millennio Adveniente*.) In his book *Crossing the Threshold of Hope* the Pope emphasizes — we should "Be Not Afraid" because mankind has been redeemed by God. He says, "The power of Christ's Cross and Resurrection is greater than any evil which man could or should fear." *He says for us to not be afraid and yet he also draws our attention to Our Lady's prophecy at Fatima in 1917 thus indicating the importance of that prophecy in relation to the world today, and what it portends for these end times if man does not return to God.*

Love and Fear the Lord

It seems to currently be the politically correct thing to do if one poohs-poohs the current emphasis on books which draw attention to the end times and the alleged doom and gloom of their contents. I witnessed one priest in a very large parish refer to those faithful who believe in La Salette, Fatima and Akita as *"doomsday dummies" and in that same breath call for his people to "shut them up." He never once distinguished between authentic Church approved apparitions and those coming from the "lunatic fringe."* He lumped them all together doing potential harm to the faithful who might then rid themselves of any notion of investigating Mary's words of warning in Her prophecies. He leaves his flock potentially out on the limb if they are not living the commandments and the beatitudes. Some priests and lay speakers shout, *"Don't let these end timers scare you; God loves you as you are."* I am certain they mean well, but this can be irresponsible if they thereby mislead the faithful by implying there is nothing to be concerned about if "Jesus loves you as you are." Those in serious and unrepentant sin have much to worry about — says Our Lady, if they should die in that state. That is why She has come!

Of course God loves us as we are — but He would hope for a change in you and me. And one can still go to hell for eternity if one dies in serious sin without repentance and this is all Our Lady is attempting to say to humanity — wake up and see that you are on the wrong road. Those leaders who reject Mary's prophetic warnings are responsible in great part for the Sunday-only Catholic not believing Her and not changing their way of life and behavior. Our Lady told Fr. Gobbi:

(328a) "... These are the painful years of the trial. This has already been foretold to you by me, in many ways and with many signs." (July 30, 1986)

Read the Sad Words of Our Blessed Mother Concerning The Mass Rejection of Her Revelations

(328b) **"But who believes me? Who listens to me? Who truly pledges himself to change his life? I am caught between two swords which pierce my motherly heart. On the one hand I see the great danger into which you are running because of the chastisement which is already at the doors (1986) ; and on the other, I see your inability to believe and to accept the invitations to conversion which I am giving you, so that you may flee from it."**

Yes, we will go to hell if we die out of friendship with God. This is a doctrine of the Church and it is in Scripture:

(219d) "The Lord is ready to pour out upon even your straying and so very threatened generation the floods of His mercy, only on condition that this generation return with repentance to the arms of its heavenly Father."

(219e) "I myself have sung of his divine mercy, which extends to all generations of men who acknowledge the Lord, *and the one and only possibility of salvation for you is in this return to the love and fear of God.*" Is there a contradiction between the words *be not afraid* and *love and fear the Lord? Not at all.* The Pope in his book on page 225 quotes from the Psalmist — "The fear of the Lord is the beginning of wisdom." (Psalm 110). He explains that fear of the Lord as a gift of the Holy Spirit has nothing to do with the fear of a slave. It is filial fear, not servile fear! The Pope says "the authentic and full expression of this fear is Christ Himself. Christ wants us to have fear of all that is an offense against God."

The Pope continues; "Every sign of servile fear vanishes before the awesome power of the All powerful and All present One. Its place is taken by filial concern in order that God's will be done on earth... Thus the Saints of every age are also an incarnation of the filial fear of Christ..." The Pope speaks of a Father-son relationship and of the respect and obedience from the son for the Father which is based on a filial fear. He says, "In order to set contemporay man free from fear of himself, of the world, of others, of earthly powers, of oppressive systems... it is necessary to pray fervently that he will bear and cultivate in his heart that true fear of God which is the beginning of wisdom."

Finally, the Pope writes, "This fear of God is the saving power of the Gospel. It is constructive, never destructive fear... It creates holy men and women — true Christians to whom the world ultimately belongs."

So we see that the Holy Father's words are not contradictory but rather they drive home the message that we need not fear the pains of hell and abandonment of God if, through our filial and respectful fear of God, we live as devout Christians in conformance with the laws of Jesus Christ! The prophecies have been given to tell us we have not been living the commandments of God and teachings of Christ. This warning is a gigantic act of mercy as is the chastisement — to save us from ourselves. Our Lady is telling us that there is not much time for the necessary changes in humanity. All the messages from La Salette, Lourdes, Fatima, Akita, etc., are messages of merciful love and are not given to frighten us into a servile and paralyzing fear of God, but to recall us to the soul-saving filial fear of the Father. Hers are words of wisdom, love and mercy for the repentant sinner, the simple, the poor, the child-like faithful remnant. Hers are words of doom and gloom only for the non-believer and the non-repentant.

CHAPTER 12

Summary and an Assumed Scenario of Events

Although it is impossible to establish a specific time-line for the events described in the period of ten years and the period from 1998 to the year 2000, it is feasible to speculate that the general sequence of events for the tribulation, chastisement, Second Pentecost, the New Times, the Second Coming, and the Day of the Lord *might be* as follows. These are my interpretations based upon Our Lady's words to Father Gobbi quoted in the book *To The Priests — Our Lady's Beloved Sons:*

1. First we consider that we are in the period of purification and tribulation at this very moment, and have been since before 1988 according to Our Lady's own words to Fr. Gobbi in Her description of the period of ten years. One visionary has stated that Jesus told her in 1943 that the world was already in the "early stages of the chastisement itself." This would indicate that the end times are actually that part of history that followed the resurrection of Jesus and that events are gradually reaching their culmination during this last century of the second millenium.

2. Next we consider the Second Pentecost, that period of the action of the Holy Spirit in a way similar to that of the first Pentecost except that He will illuminate the entire world. This world-wide reawakening will follow immediately after the Warning wherein Mary says we will all see our souls as God sees us in a kind of miniature judgement. This experience gives mankind a second chance to convert to the living of the Gospels and a return to God. Many will convert and the good will grow in holiness. These will constitute the REMNANT, in whose hearts and souls the Reign of Christ will take place. This constitutes His Second Coming in glory. He will show Himself to many as He was seen at the time of the Ascencion in His glorified body. This Second Coming takes place before His FINAL coming for the last judgement. *Only God the Father knows the time of the FINAL COMING.* The Second Coming, therefore, is for the new Reign of Christ on earth in the hearts of the relatively few members of the remnant. The FINAL COMING is for the final judgement of all at the end of the world. Read here the words of Mary to Father Gobbi on December 24, 1978. These words are of extreme importance for a clear understanding of the Second Coming as opposed to the FINAL COMING of the Lord:

(166e) "His second coming, beloved children, will be like the first. As was his birth on this night, so also will be the return of Jesus in glory, *BEFORE* HIS FINAL COMING FOR THE LAST JUDGEMENT, the hour of which, however, is still hidden in the secrets of the Father.

(166f) "The world will be completely covered in darkness of the denial of God, of the obstinate rejection of Him and of rebellion against his law of love. The coldness of hatred will still cause the roadways of this world to be deserted. Almost no one will be ready to receive Him."

(166g) "The great ones will not even remember Him, the rich will close their doors on Him, while his own will be too busy with seeking and affirming themselves..."

(166i) "Even in this second coming, the Son will come to you through his Mother... *so also will Jesus make use of my Immaculate Heart to come and reign in your midst.*"

(166j) "This is the hour of my Immaculate Heart because the coming of Jesus' glorious reign of love is now in preparation."

NOTE: I draw your attention to par166h in Fr. Gobbi's book, if you have one in your possession. I am not including it here because, if my reading of it is correct, there appears to be a contradiction or misprint in that paragraph in the book, and I do not want to introduce confusion. Paragraphs 166i and 166j, immediately above, however, clarify the apparent contradiction as it appears to me in the book.

3. Next we consider that the reawakening, the Second Pentecost, will prepare the remnant who will survive the culmination of the chastisement, which serves as a punishment and a cleansing of the world. This survival will be a spiritual survival for those who resisted the actions of an Anti-Pope who will be under the inspiration of Satan at work in the world and in the Church itself. The Anti-Christ might be active in some manner working through the Anti-Pope. But the full fury of the Anti-Christ will be manifested at some time after the great period of peace that will follow the chastisement. In other words, the Anti-Christ will function supremely in the world just immediately before the end of the world and after the period of peace. Some of the remnant will survive the chastisement physically as well, while many of the remnant will be martyred as saints. The reprobates will not survive spiritually but will be lost souls through their own choice, and will suffer a bodily death in the chastise-

ment — that "fire that will fall from heaven." The Triumph of Mary's Immaculate Heart will become manifest in the hearts and souls of the faithful who will live intimately with Christ although persecuted and martyred. They will withstand the heresies and the errors and betrayals of the Anti-Pope because they will have found refuge under the mantle of the Blessed Mother for their spiritual safety.

At the time of the chastisement, that apocalyptic form of punishment, in whatever form it comes, will rid the earth of the wicked and Satan with his fallen angels. Some of the remnant will die as well, but will die as martyrs and will enter heaven.

4. Next we consider that after the chastisement, which will result in the death of millions, the surviving remnant will live through a period of world desolation, but gradually there will be on earth the time of peace during which all on earth will accept the Catholic Faith and follow the Holy Father of that time. The sick will be healed and this will be the time of unity and a" new heaven and a new earth." A great brotherhood, peace and the virtues will mark life on the new earth. Satan will have been defeated and the New Times on earth will support the surviving remnant with a life that will duplicate the kind of life as was once in the Garden of Eden. This might be the time that Pope John Paul II thinks will take place starting in the year 2000, the time he describes as the New Springtime of the Church. Some writers think this will last for two or three generations after which man will succumb once again to pride and even a greater loss of faith than during the period of ten years. During this new period of apostasy, the reign of the real Anti-Christ will be a period of abject horror on earth — a living hell on earth. This time will include a terrible persecution of all Christians up through the time of the three days of darkness which

will immediately precede the real "end of the world" and the *final* coming of Christ for the Last Judgement.

I point out to the reader again that the locutions to Fr. Gobbi are allegedly from Our Blessed Mother and I use exclusively Her words from his book to draw my conclusions above. There are various interpretations of other prophets in print, but in my opinion, the words of Mary quoted here provide a reasonable expectation for our future and the possible sequence of events. Even if the events occur in a different manner from the above interpretation of Our Lady's words to Fr. Gobbi, we must admit that Her words provide wise and prudent counsel to the faithful.

The Virgin Mary, Fr. Gobbi and the Year 2000

CHAPTER 13

The Thoughts of a Highly Respected and Well-Informed Author on the End Times

In my research for this book I acquired a copy of the excellent book by Mr. Ralph Martin, titled *Is Jesus Coming Soon? A Catholic Perspective on the Second Coming (1997)*. I believe it is one of the best books on the market for an easy but informative read on this topic. Mr. Martin is the head of Renewal Ministries, Ann Arbor, Michigan and has a regular program on Mother Angelica's EWTN Television Network where his book was discussed.

My approach to the discussion of this topic was to confine the material, for the most part, to Our Lady's words in Fr. Gobbi's book, *To The Priests — Our Lady's Beloved Sons*. Mr. Martin's book delves deeply into the Scriptures and what they hold for the end-times, although he quotes from Fr. Gobbi as well in his Chapter Nine, pp. 147-148. For the scriptural foundation of the Catholic perspective on the end times his book is a must, in my opinion, for anyone interested in or speaking about the end times. As a matter of fact, the reason he wrote his book was to help clarify, at the request of many, the interpretation and meaning of the recent locutions and apparitions that commented on the end times and how they mesh with Scripture. I now quote from Mr. Martin's book:

" ...This upsurge in prophetic activity and the manifestation of charismatic gifts of the Spirit in both Catholic and Protestant circles is unprecedented, in my opinion, since the early days of the Church. In the Catholic Church the Marian form of a major stream of prophetic activity is also unprecedented in its frequency and extent. Much of the prophetic activity speaks of very critical years ahead of us involving purification, tribulation, possible chastisement, as well as a great outpouring of grace and mercy on the world, ushering in either the return of Jesus Himself or at least a 'new springtime of Christianity.'" (p149.)

... I would be very cautious in approaching messages such as those Fr. Gobbi claims to have received from Mary concerning the return of Jesus in 1998 or 2000. This seems perilously close to specifying the return of the Lord in a way that is not compatible with the spirit of Jesus' warning to the contrary and not harmonious with the other messages of Mary in much more solidly attested communications. Our prophecy, like our knowledge, is currently imperfect (1 Cor 13:9). which isn't to say that either is not valuable; valuable, just not perfect.

It seems to me that, compared to the rest of Christian history, our time could be fairly described as fulfilling better than any other time the scriptural warnings about the mass apostasy and the removal of the restrainer on lawlessness. Yet, we have to remember that if the Lord does not come soon, a future time of Christian history may even better fulfill these wretched realities than we do today. God forbid!

The most valuable part of this book, I believe, are the chapters that outline what the Scriptures really say about the Lord's return and the events that accompany it, within the context of the basic message of salvation and redemption, and the implications for daily Christian life. And yet it is only reasonable for readers to ask, as they have done periodically over the years, what I think about these Scripture's applicability to our time. Let me tell you, very simply.

I think that these years we are living in are very special times in the history both of the world and of the Church. The conflict between good and evil is intensifying, in what appears to be merely human and what appears to be more than human. In my judgement, the mutiplicity of angel sightings is not just a new age fad. Forces are gathering; the battle is intensifying. Great mercy and grace are being offered to the human race in so many ways. And great evil is unfolding. The pressure on youth today is almost unbearable.

I think it is hard to exaggerate the significance of the activity of Mary in recent years and the reappearance on a widespread scale of the charisms of the Holy Spirit not seen in this way since the early Church. Something very special is being offered the human race: an opportunity to repent, to believe, to turn to God. An opportunity for eternal life. I think it's very possible, as St... Louis de Montfort prophesied, that the twentieth century will be known as the Age of Mary and the Age of the Holy Spirit. And just as God in his unfathomable wisdom chose Mary to prepare for the Lord's First Coming, so he is sending her again to prepare for the Lord's Second Coming, using her to raise up apostles and prophets for the last days.

And yet perhaps what we are seeing unfold around us is not yet the last days in the sense of the time immediately before the

Lord's return. Perhaps what we are seeing is the preparation and unfolding of the end of an age: the end of two thousand years of Christiandom and the return of the Church to an existence like she had in the early centuries, a minority body in the midst of a pagan empire, yet full of faith, hope, and love, the gospel spreading, Christ triumphing even in the apparent defeat of his disciples. Perhaps what we are seeing is preparation, not for the final harvest, but yet for something nonetheless wonderful, a new springtime of Christianity, where currently divided Christians find themselves closer together as they witness together to him in the midst of a lawless, anti-Christian world. God again using the weak things of the world, things the world despises, to confound the wisdom of the world, so that in the days to come faith might not rest just on words or formulas but on the power of God manifested in Word and Spirit.

Is Jesus coming soon? I don't know. He very well might be; many signs point to it. But whether or not he comes in the next few years, it certainly seems as if we're in for some very special times. Chastisement, tribulation, purification, mercy, renewal, revival, repentance, new evangelization, new Pentecost, reconciliation, new springtime, are somehow, I believe, all part of the picture.

But whether or not he comes in the next few years, or even whether or not the new springtime comes, is not the most significant thing. The most significant thing is that Jesus is the same yesterday, today, and forever and that we can know and love him now and follow him, no matter what happens or doesn't happen in the world and Church around us. He surely is present now and wanting to come to each and every one of us as we open our hearts and minds to him and surrender to the grace he offers us all. He is coming. He is truly coming in so many ways to all of us. In the signs he gives us in the daily experience of our life. In his word. In 'chance encounters.' In his servants. In the poor, the sick, the handicapped. In the unexpected. In the neighbor of the moment. In the gentle power of the sacraments. In the cleansing of reconciliation, in the unfathomable love and intimacy of Eucharist, in the mystery and sign of marriage, in the abiding presence of orders, in the new birth of Baptism and Confirmation, in the comfort and healing of anointing. In our hearts always, dwelling within us, Father, Son, and Holy Spirit..." (pp. 150-154 of Mr. Martin's book)

Mr. Martin cites in his book a number of alleged locutions of Our Lady concerning the period of ten years from Fr. Gobbi's book and he seems to accept and agree with those words although he cautions us to be careful about expecting the Second Coming of Jesus in any specific year. Good advice. I suspect, however, that a very special time is around the corner during these years before 2000 in view of Satan's grip on the world during this century. Considering the promise of Mary, that her Immaculate Heart will triumph by the year 2000, can we imagine what these years might bring even if the Second Coming is well off into the future? A merciful Mother is warning us to always be prepared for our particular judgement for we know not when it comes for each of us, but Mary promises we will find refuge in Her Immaculate Heart and the infinite Mercy of Jesus.

May God bless you, and draw you ever nearer to Himself. May you receive the gifts of wisdom and holy fear of the Lord. I pray that all who read the Bible, *the Catechism of the Catholic Church*, and live the eucharistic life, will also strive to be a hero for Christ — a member of THE REMNANT!